# The best of
# Akbar-Birbal

An imprint of Om Books International

Reprinted in 2015

An imprint of Om Books International

Corporate & Editorial Office
A 12, Sector 64, Noida 201 301
Uttar Pradesh, India
Phone: +91 120 477 4100
Email: editorial@ombooks.com
Website: www.ombooksinternational.com

Sales Office
107, Darya Ganj, New Delhi 110 002, India
Phone: +91 11 4000 9000, 2326 3363, 2326 5303
Fax: +91 11 2327 8091
Email: sales@ombooks.com
Website: www.ombooks.com

ISBN: 978-93-80069-32-6

Printed in India

1 0 9 8 7 6 5

# Contents

# How Akbar Met Birbal

Emperor Akbar loved hunting. One day while hunting, Akbar and some of the courtiers went so fast that they left the others behind. As the evening fell, they realised that they had lost their way and did not know where to go. They were tired, hungry and thirsty too, by then.

At last they came to a junction of three roads. The Emperor was very happy to see the roads but neither he nor his courtiers knew which road led to his capital, Agra. As they were all thinking about it, they saw a young man coming along one of the roads.

The man was summoned. Akbar asked him, "Hey, young man! Which of these roads goes to Agra?" The man smiled and answered, "Everybody knows that roads cannot move, so how would these roads go to Agra or anywhere else?"

Everybody was silent for a minute, and then Akbar laughed and said, "You are right!" And asked, "What is your name, young man?" "Mahesh Das," the man replied and asked the Emperor, "And who are you? What is your name?"

The Emperor took off one of his rings and gave it to the man. "You are talking to Emperor Akbar, the King of

Hindustan. We need fearless people like you in our country. Now tell me the way to get to Agra. We have to reach there soon."

Mahesh Das pointed towards the road going to Agra, and the King and his courtiers headed on that road back home.

This is how Emperor Akbar met the future Birbal.

# Mahesh Das Becomes Birbal

Mahesh Das had completed his studies. He was a young man, looking for a job, when he remembered his chance meeting with Emperor Akbar a couple of years ago. He decided to go and meet him. So he took all his savings,

along with the ring which he received from the Emperor himself, bade his mother farewell, and set out to the new capital of India - Fatehpur Sikri.

Mahesh Das was impressed with the pomp and show of the capital, as he headed towards the red walls of the palace. The huge palace gates were guarded. Mahesh wanted to enter the gate, but the guard stopped him.

"Where do you think you are going?" asked the guard.

Mahesh replied politely, "Sir, I have come to see the King."

"And the King must be waiting for you, isn't it?" the guard said sarcastically.

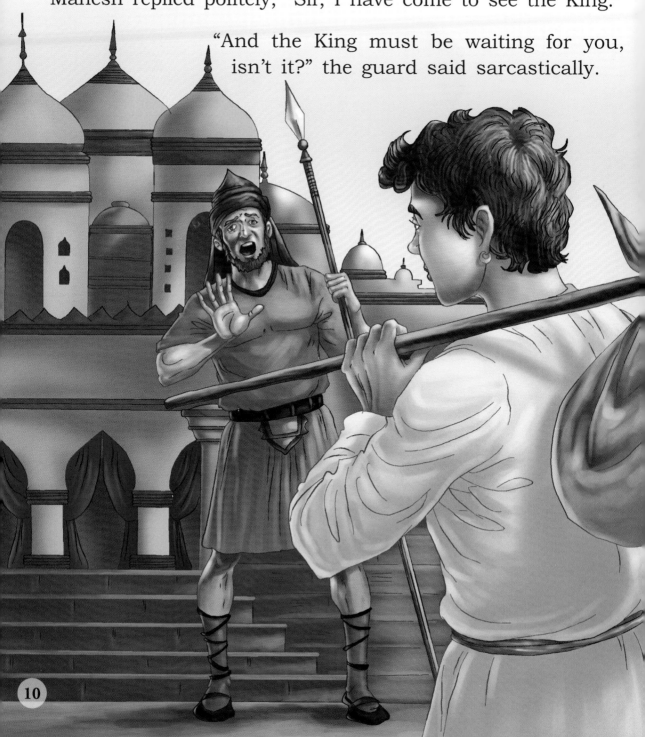

Mahesh smiled at this comment and said, "Yes, Sir. And now I am here."

The guard became angry and shouted, "No one can just walk in to see the Emperor! Go away before I chop off your head!"

Mahesh was not going to accept his defeat. He showed Akbar's ring to the guard. Everyone in the kingdom recognised the royal ring. Having seen it, the guard could not say a word. He had to allow Mahesh in, although he was still unwilling to do so.

So the guard thought and said to Mahesh, "You can go in on one condition, whatever you will get from the Emperor, you must share with me half of that."

Mahesh agreed and the guard let him go inside.

Mahesh Das went in and prostrated himself before the great Emperor. Akbar smiled and asked, "What do you want, young man?"

Mahesh rose to his feet and spoke, "Sir, I have come here at your command," and showed the ring.

Akbar recognised the ring and said, "Welcome young man! Now tell me, what is your heart's desire? I will try my best to fulfill it."

Mahesh remembered his promise to the guard, so he asked the Emperor to punish him with one hundred whiplashes.

The King was surprised to hear that, "But how can I do this to you? You have done nothing wrong!"

Mahesh said politely, "Sir, please do not go back from your promise of fulfilling my heart's desire."

So with great reluctance, Akbar ordered one hundred lashes on Mahesh's back. To the surprise of all, Mahesh endured every stroke without uttering a word. After the fiftieth whip, he suddenly shouted, "Stop now!"

Akbar asked, "Why? What happened?"

Mahesh said, "Sir when I was coming here, your guard did not allow me to come inside the palace, unless I promised him to give half of my share of whatever I get from you. I have taken half of my share, now it is your guard's turn to take his share of half."

Everybody burst into laughter. The guard was called in to receive his humiliating bribe.

The King said, "You are as brave as you were before. You have grown into a clever young man. I was trying to weed out the corrupt people from my court, but your little trick has done what I couldn't have done even after passing several laws. From now on, on the basis of your wisdom, you shall be called 'Birbal' and you will stay by my side as my advisor."

That is how Birbal was born.

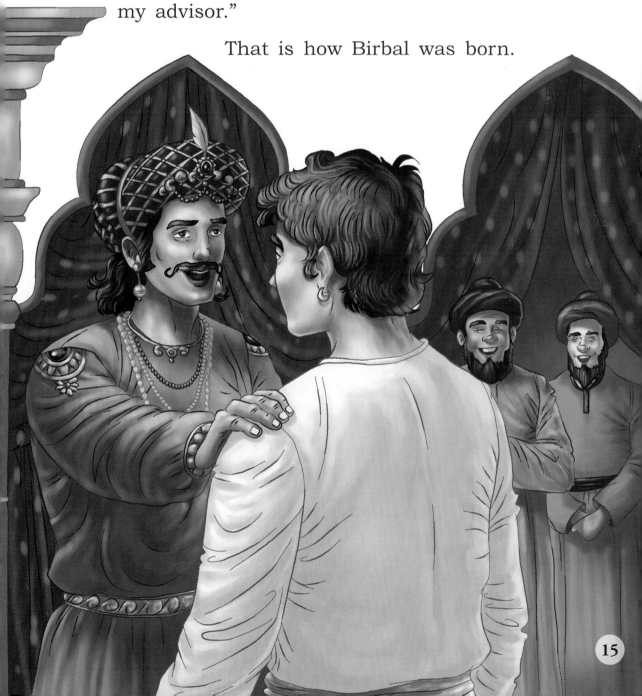

# A Question for a Question

Emperor Akbar loved talking to Birbal. Often he would ask Birbal questions, just to hear him come up with witty answers.

One day as they were strolling in the royal gardens, Akbar asked Birbal a question.

"Birbal, can you tell me, how many bangles are there on your wife's wrists?"

"No, I am afraid I do not know," Birbal replied.

"How can you not? I am sure that you see her every day, yet you do not notice!"

"Come with me, and I will tell you why I do not know," Birbal suggested to Akbar.

Birbal then led Akbar towards the stairs leading inside the palace. As they reached the top of the stairs, Birbal asked Akbar, how many stairs had they climbed?

"I have never noticed, so I cannot tell you," Akbar replied.

"But, you climb these stairs every day, yet it escaped your notice!" Birbal said to Akbar.

Akbar smiled and changed the subject, as he thought to that the clever Birbal seemed to know all the answers!

# The Real Donkey

One day, Akbar took Birbal along with his two sons to the river to bathe.

As they reached the river, Akbar and his sons took off their clothes and handed them to Birbal, saying, "Take good care of them, while we bathe."

As Emperor Akbar bathed in the river, he saw Birbal standing in the corner holding their clothes.

Birbal looked an odd sight and so the jovial King could not resist the urge to tease him.

"Birbal! You look like a washerman's donkey carrying all that load!" Akbar called out, laughing loudly.

"Huzoor, a washerman's donkey only carries one donkey's load and here I am carrying three donkeys' load!" Birbal exclaimed.

# The Camel's Crooked Neck

Emperor Akbar enjoyed talking to Birbal and listening to his quick wit. One day Akbar was especially pleased with Birbal and said to him, "Birbal, for your wisdom and wit, I promise to reward you with many beautiful and valuable gifts!" Birbal was very pleased.

Several days passed and there was no sign of the gifts that Akbar had promised. Birbal was quite disappointed. He thought to himself, "Surely the great Emperor would not go back on his word! I must remind him somehow."

One day as Akbar and Birbal were walking down the bank of river Yamuna, they saw a camel. Akbar stopped and asked, "Why is the camel's neck crooked?"

Birbal knew this was his chance to remind the king. He said, "Sir, I think it is because the camel forgot to honour a promise that he had made. It says so in the scriptures too, if you do not honour a promise you are punished with a crooked neck!"

Akbar realised his mistake at once. The very next day, he rewarded Birbal with many valuable gifts.

As always, Birbal managed to get what he wanted, without asking for it directly!

# Birbal Catches the Thief

Birbal's wisdom was known far and wide in the city of Agra. Often people would come to him with their problems.

One day, a rich merchant paid a visit to Birbal. His house had been robbed, and he suspected that one of his servants had committed the robbery. So, the merchant invited Birbal to come to his house.

Birbal agreed, and the next day, he visited the merchant's house early in the morning.

He called all the merchant's servants one by one and questioned them. All of them denied of robbing the merchant.

Birbal then called all of them together and handed them each a stick of equal length.

"These sticks are magical. They will instantly know who the thief is. The stick which is owned by the thief will grow two inches over the night; so make sure to get them back tomorrow morning." Birbal instructed the servants.

The next day, Birbal went to the merchant's house to collect the sticks. He asked the servants to show their sticks. One of them was shorter than the others.

Birbal immediately knew who the thief was. Pointing at the servant, he explained to the merchant that in the fear that his stick would grow two inches overnight, the thief had foolishly cut it two inches shorter. And the sticks were really just ordinary sticks!

# Birbal Returns

One day, when Akbar and Birbal were talking, Birbal passed a harmless comment about Akbar himself. But since Emperor Akbar was not in a good mood, he got angry on Birbal's remark. He asked him to not only leave the palace, but also to leave the city of Agra.

A couple of days later, Akbar began to miss Birbal. He regretted his earlier decision of sending him away, so sent out a search party to look for him. But Birbal had left the city, without telling anybody where he was going. The soldiers searched everywhere, but were unable to find him.

Then one day a holy man came to visit the palace accompanied by two of his disciples. The holy man had bright sparkling eyes, a thick beard and long hair. The disciples claimed that their teacher was the wisest man on Earth. Since Akbar was missing Birbal's advice, he thought it would be a good idea to have a wise man as an advisor. But he decided that he would first test the holy man's wisdom.

The next day, when the holy man and his disciples came to visit the court, Akbar informed him that he would like to test him. All his ministers would put forward a question and if his

answers were satisfactory, he would be made a minister. But if he could not answer, then he would be beheaded. The holy man answered that he had never claimed to be the wisest man on Earth, even though other people seemed to think so. Nor was he eager to display his cleverness, but as he enjoyed answering questions, he was ready for the test.

One of the ministers, Raja Todarmal, began the round of questioning. He asked, "Who is a man's best friend on Earth?" To which the wise man replied, "His own good sense". Next Faizi asked, "Which is the most superior thing on Earth?" "Knowledge", answered the man. "What is that which cannot be regained after it is lost?" questioned another courtier and the reply he received was, "Life". The court musician Tansen asked, "Which is the sweetest and most melodious voice at night-time?" And the answer he received was, "The voice that prays to God."

Maharaj Mansingh of Jaipur, who was a guest at the palace asked, "What travels faster than the wind?" The holy man replied that it was "Man's thought". He then asked, "Which is the sweetest thing on Earth?" And the man said that it was "A baby's smile".

Emperor Akbar was very impressed with all the answers, but wanted to test the holy man himself. He asked, "What is the necessary requirement to rule over a kingdom?" For which he was answered "Cleverness". Then he asked, "Who is the biggest enemy of a king?" The man replied that it is "Selfishness".

The Emperor was pleased and offered the holy man a seat of honour and finally asked him whether he could perform any miracles. The saint said that he could manifest any person the king wished to meet. Akbar was thrilled and immediately asked to meet his minister and best friend Birbal.

The holy man simply pulled off his artificial beard and hair, much to the surprise of the other courtiers. Akbar could not believe his eyes! He stepped down to embrace the man, because he was none other than Birbal! He showered Birbal with many valuable gifts to show him how happy he was at his return.

# Honest Birbal

One fine day, Emperor Akbar was discussing the vegetable brinjal with Birbal. He said it was a delicious vegetable, good for health and the best among all vegetables. Much to Akbar's surprise, Birbal also thoroughly agreed with him, and even sang two songs in praise of the humble brinjal.

After a couple of days, the royal chef cooked brinjal curry for lunch. Birbal was also eating at the palace that day. When the brinjal curry was served to Akbar, he refused it, saying that it was a tasteless, unhealthy vegetable, full of seeds. He then asked that it be served to Birbal who loved brinjals. But Birbal too, refused it, saying that it was certainly not good for health.

Akbar was surprised at Birbal's reaction. He asked him why he was saying such things when he sang the brinjal's praise, just a few days ago. How could he have two opposite opinions for the same thing?

Birbal replied that he had praised the brinjal only because his Emperor had praised it and criticised it when his Emperor had criticised it, as he was loyal to his Emperor and not to the brinjal. He said that the brinjal could not make him a minister no matter how much he praised it! Akbar was pleased by Birbal's honest, bold, and witty response.

# Birbal Goes to Heaven

Birbal was very wise and witty, and Emperor Akbar's favourite. This made the other courtiers jealous of him, and they were always trying to find ways to make him look foolish.

One day the court barber, who was very jealous of Birbal, plotted a plan against him. Akbar called him to trim his beard. As the barber started trimming the Emperor's beard, he said, "Sir, last night I dreamed about your father." The Emperor got interested, so he asked, "What did he say to you?"

"Sir, he said to me, that everything is good in paradise, but he feels the absence of a good humorous man who can amuse him."

Akbar thought hard, but nobody else could he think of except Birbal who could perform this kind of duty very well. And, naturally, the only way to go to heaven was through death. For a moment, Akbar was very sad to lose such a good man, but thinking of his father, he made up his mind.

He summoned Birbal and said, "I think Birbal, you love me very much and can sacrifice anything for me." Birbal replied, "You know Majesty, I do."

"Then Birbal, please go to heaven to give company to my dear father." Birbal realised that this was a wicked plan of somebody to kill him. He said to the Emperor politely, "I will do so, but I need a few days to prepare myself to go to heaven." Akbar said, "Certainly. I will allow you one week to prepare yourself."

Birbal went back home and thought about the whole thing. Somebody had planned very well and it seemed he could not escape from this plan. But then, Birbal found a way. He dug a ditch near his house which would serve as his grave, and dug a tunnel too which would open in a room of his house. After doing this, he returned to the court.

Birbal told Akbar, "I am ready, Your Majesty, but there are two conditions." Akbar was so happy to hear this that he did not mind whatever conditions Birbal might have had. He asked, "Tell me the conditions. I will try to fulfill them, so that you can go to heaven to be with my dear father, soon."

Birbal said, "I wish to be buried near my house. And I want to be buried alive so that I can reach heaven alive to amuse your dear father." Akbar found this to be sensible and agreed immediately.

So Birbal was buried alive near his house. He immediately made his way into the house where he lived in hiding for six months. After six months, he came out with a fully-grown beard and shabby hair and went straight to the royal court.

Looking at him Akbar cried, "How have you been Birbal?" Birbal answered, "Your Majesty, I was in heaven with your dear father. I had a very good time there with him. He was so happy with my services that he gave me special permission to return to Earth."

"Did he send any message for me?" Akbar was anxious to know. Birbal said, "Yes Your Majesty, he said that very few barbers are able to go to heaven, as you can make out from my grown beard and shabby hair. So he has asked to send your own barber to him immediately."

Akbar understood everything. He gave Birbal a reward, and his barber the life sentence.

# Crows in the Kingdom

One day Emperor Akbar and Birbal were taking a walk in the palace gardens. It was a nice summer morning and there were plenty of crows happily playing around the pond.

While watching the crows, a question came into Akbar's mind. He wondered how many crows were there in his kingdom. Since Birbal was accompanying him, he asked Birbal this question.

After a moment's thought, Birbal replied, "There are ninety-five thousand, four hundred and sixty-three crows in the Kingdom."

Amazed by his quick response, Akbar tried to test him again, "What if there are more crows than you answered?" Without hesitating Birbal replied, "If there are more crows than my answer, then some crows are visiting from other neighbouring kingdoms."

"And what if there are less crows?" Akbar asked. "Then some crows from our kingdom have gone on holiday to other places!"

# The Royal Advisor

Akbar's many courtiers were competing with each other to become the Emperor's royal advisor. One day they all decided to go to Akbar. They requested, "Your Majesty, you must choose the person who will take on the position of being your royal advisor."

"Fine, but you first have to pass a test." Akbar replied.

As he said that, Akbar undid his royal robe and kept it on the floor. He then told his courtiers that the person who would be able to cover him entirely with his robe would become the royal advisor.

Every courtier tried, but none was successful. If they managed to cover his torso, they would leave his feet bare. When they had almost given up, Birbal entered.

"Birbal, why don't you give it a try?" Akbar called out to him.

Birbal at once took the royal robe and said to Akbar, "Your Majesty, could you please bend down a little?"

As Akbar bent his knees, the robe covered his entire body. Akbar happily gave the position of his royal advisor to Birbal.

As for the courtiers, they were too ashamed to ever ask for the position of the royal advisor again!

# Flowers for Akbar

One day, Akbar and his courtiers were walking in the palace gardens. It was the season of spring and many beautiful flowers were blooming. As they walked, a poet from Akbar's court pointed towards a flower and exclaimed, "Oh look Your Majesty! Such a beautiful sight that flower is! No man can produce an equal to this!"

Birbal was also among the courtiers. He immediately spoke up, saying, "I am afraid I do not agree!"

"Do not be silly, Birbal! The poet is right, man can never produce anything as beautiful as this spring flower," Akbar said firmly.

A week from this incident, Birbal presented Akbar with a bouquet of beautifully carved flowers. They were made by the most skilled craftsman in the whole of Agra city. Pleased with his gift, Akbar rewarded the craftsman with a thousand gold coins.

Just then a little boy came to Akbar and gave him a beautiful real flower. Akbar was quite pleased to receive it too, so he gave the boy one gold coin.

Just as Akbar was handing the boy the coin, Birbal commented, "I was right after all! Man can make something more beautiful than the lovely spring flowers in your garden."

Akbar laughed loudly. He was once again caught by his witty minister!

# Birbal's Sweet Reply

Akbar would often ask his courtiers odd questions. Their replies would amuse him greatly.

One day he walked into his court with an interesting question. "Tell me, what would you do to the person who dares to pull my moustache?" Akbar asked loudly.

Many courtiers had answers and Akbar listened to them patiently. Some courtiers said:

"Your Majesty, the one who dares to insult you in such fashion, should be hanged!"

"No, no! I say he should be run down by elephants!"

"The scoundrel should be flogged, I say!"

Another said, "Perhaps he should get a hundred blows on his back!"

But Akbar was dissatisfied with all the answers.

Birbal was sitting quietly when Akbar said to him, "Birbal, have you got nothing to add? What do you think should be done to the person who pulls my moustache?"

"Your Majesty, I think the person should be given sweets!"

"Birbal, did you not understand the question? How could you even dare to suggest such a thing?" Akbar exclaimed angrily.

"I dare to suggest this, because no one other than your own grandson would do such a thing. Now you would not want him flogged in the streets, would you?"

Akbar was so pleased with Birbal's reply, that he gave him one of his royal rings.

# Birbal Identifies the Guest

Once Birbal was invited for supper by a rich man. The rich man had heard of Birbal's intelligence and he wanted to see if Birbal was indeed as clever as people thought him to be.

When Birbal reached the rich man's home, he saw a huge gathering of people. Birbal greeted the host and remarked, "I did not know that there would be so many guests!"

"These are my servants in disguise. Among them is the other gentleman who will be accompanying us for supper. Perhaps you could identify him."

"Perhaps I could, if you would tell them a joke!"

Puzzled by Birbal's request, the host told the gathering a joke. It was probably the worst joke in the world, yet everyone laughed loudly.

Birbal immediately pointed towards one gentleman in the corner, saying, "There is your other guest!"

The host was baffled, "How did you get to know?"

"It was simple. All your servants laughed, in fear of offending you by not laughing, while your guest did not even as much as smile."

"Ah, Birbal, you truly are as clever and intelligent as people claim you to be! I am greatly honoured to be in your company!" the host replied, smiling.

# Distance between Truth and Lie

Akbar frequently had question-and-answer sessions in his court. He would ask his courtiers some questions, and the ones with the best answers would be rewarded.

One day, Akbar wanted to know the distance between a truth and a lie. Akbar's courtiers were puzzled; they thought and thought, but none could come up with a fitting answer.

Finally Birbal spoke up, "Four fingers, Your Majesty."

"What are you saying Birbal?" Akbar asked Birbal.

"What we see with our eyes is always the truth, but often what we hear is a lie."

"That is true, but what has it got to do with four fingers?"

"Your Majesty, four fingers is the distance between your eyes and your ears." Birbal said, astonishing Akbar with his answer.

# Four Fools

Once Akbar asked Birbal to bring him four of the world's worst possible fools. So the following morning, Birbal began looking for the fools.

The first fool he saw was a Brahmin. This Brahmin was running very fast carrying a plate of betel-nut, rice and a few other things. When the Minister asked the Brahmin why he was running, the Brahmin answered, "My wife has just given birth to a son, and I am bringing her the ceremonial foods. Unfortunately, the boy is not my child, but his father will also be there.

So I am going to bless the new father and mother, and the baby. That is why I am running."

"Ah!" thought the Minister, "I have got my first fool," and he told the Brahmin to come to the court with him.

"No, no! I cannot come to the court," protested the Brahmin. "I have to go to my wife."

Birbal declared, "I am the Emperor's Minister. It is the Emperor's command that you come." So the foolish Brahmin had to go to Akbar's palace.

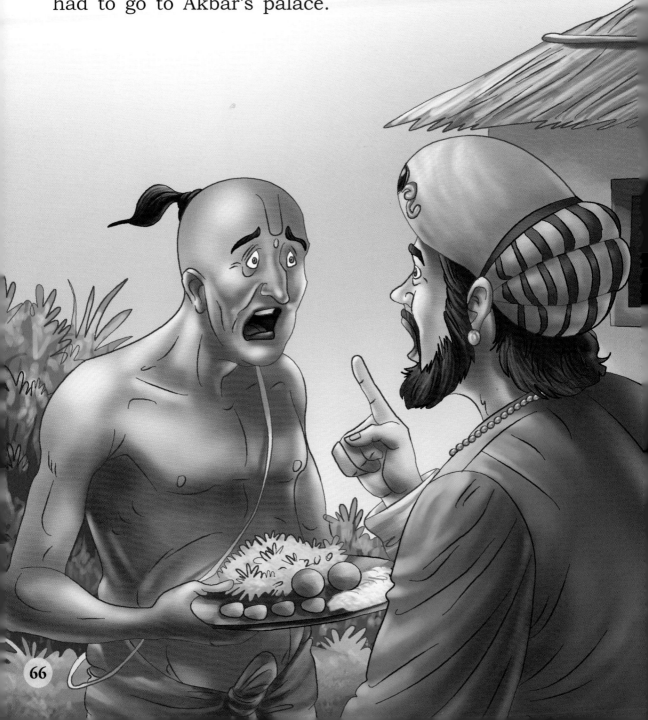

On the way, they saw a man sitting on a horse. The man was carrying a very heavy load on his shoulders. Birbal asked him, "Why are you carrying that load on your shoulders?"

The man replied, "My horse is a mare, and she is pregnant. I do not want to hurt this poor animal by making her carry such a heavy burden, so I have put the load on my own shoulders."

Birbal said, "If you are sitting on the horse, the weight will be the same whether it is on your shoulders or on the back of the horse." But the man insisted that he was taking half the burden on his own shoulders.

"Here is another fool," Birbal said to himself, and commanded the man to come along to the Emperor.

"Your Majesty," proclaimed the Minister when they came before Akbar, "here are your fools."

"I asked you to bring me four fools, did I not?" said Akbar. "Where are the other two?"

"I have two here," replied Birbal, and he narrated their foolish actions to the Emperor.

Then he said, "The third fool is you, Your Majesty. Who but a fool is interested in seeing fools? A wise Emperor would like to know whether there are wise men in his Empire. And I am the fourth fool. I listen to your foolish commands and waste my time carrying them out. Only a fool would obey the commands of a fool, so that makes me the fourth fool."

# The Potter's Dream

There was once a poor potter in the city of Agra. He made pots and earned barely enough to support his family. But no matter how difficult it was, he and his wife always managed to feed themselves and their children. The potter was proud of the fact that he had never borrowed a single copper coin. "We must never fall into the hands of the moneylender," he often told his wife, "for if we do, we would surely be ruined."

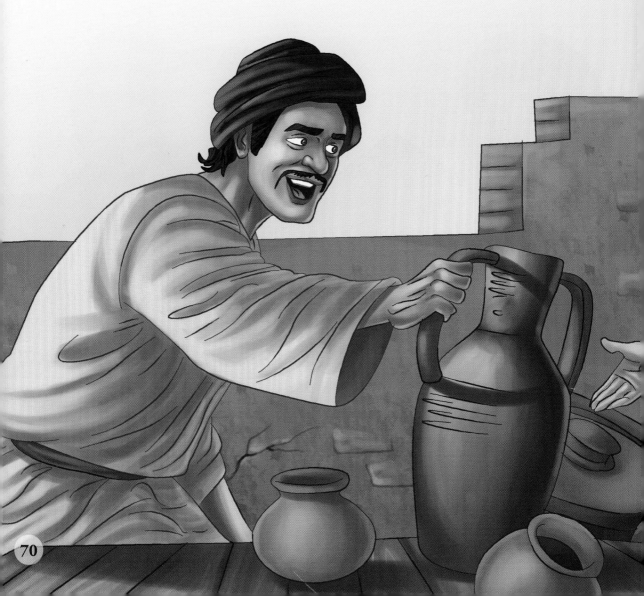

The potter worried so much about his lack of money and his fear of borrowing, that his worries even found a place in his dreams. One night, he dreamt that he had borrowed one hundred gold coins from the moneylender. He woke up in terror, thinking, "One hundred gold coins! Where, oh where will I ever find such wealth?" Still trembling from his nightmare, he woke his wife and told her all about it.

The next day, as the potter's wife drew water from the well, she told her friends of her husband's dream. "Imagine!" she exclaimed. "He dreamt that we had borrowed not one or two, but one hundred gold coins from the moneylender!" Her friends laughed with her. A few of them thought it was a very good story and repeated it to their husbands when they got home.

The story spread and a few days later, it reached the moneylender's ears. He laughed when he heard it, but his eyes began to glitter greedily. That evening, he put on his turban and, picking up his walking stick strolled over to the potter's house.

"I have come," he announced to the nervous and worried potter, "to remind you of the money you owe me."

"Money?" cried the potter in panic. "I owe you?"

"Yes," answered the moneylender firmly. "One hundred gold coins. Surely you have not forgotten?"

"One-one-one h-h-hundred gold coins..." stammered the potter, nearly fainting.

The potter's wife, who had been listening from inside the house, came hurrying out. "But it was only a

dream!" she cried. "You cannot ask us to return money that has only been borrowed in a dream!"

"Money is money," the moneylender said, "and money borrowed must be returned. You will have to start tomorrow. I am a kind man, a good-hearted man, and so I shall not demand it all back at once. One gold coin a month will do. And then, there will be the interest above that as well." And with these words, he stood up and left.

The potter and his wife sat in despair. Suddenly, the wife had an idea, "We must request Birbal to help us. Only he can save us from ruin." At this, the potter sat up. Strength and energy seemed to flow into his limbs. "I shall go to his house at once," he said. "If anyone can save us it is he."

Birbal listened to the poor potter's tale. Then he brought out a bag of gold coins and emptied them on to a table. He counted out a hundred and put the rest away. Then he placed a large mirror in front of the coins.

"Sir!" the potter said in a distressed voice. "I did not come here to beg you to pay the moneylender. Surely there is another way!"

"Yes there is," Birbal answered with a smile. "Go and call the moneylender to my house. Tell him his debt is about to be paid."

The potter hurried to the moneylender's house with Birbal's message. The moneylender smiled when he heard this and got up at once to accompany him.

When they arrived at Birbal's house and were shown in, the moneylender spotted the pile of gold coins on the table. He smiled, unable to take his eyes off them. The mirror behind the coins made the pile look larger and more glittering.

"So the potter borrowed a hundred gold coins from you in his dream, did he?"

"That is so," replied the moneylender, never taking his eyes off the coins on the table.

"Well," said Birbal. "You may take all the coins in the mirror," said Birbal. The real coins belong to me, but all those in the reflection are yours in return for the dream loan!"

The moneylender knew he had met his match. Without a word, he turned and left the house. Never again did he try to bully the potter or anyone else in the city of Agra.

# Birbal's Beautiful Explanation

One day, Emperor Akbar saw a woman kissing a very ugly child. As he observed them, he remarked to Birbal, "Look at that woman Birbal; how she caresses that child as if it is the most beautiful child in the world."

"Your Majesty, that child must be hers. To every mother, her child is the most beautiful one in the world."

However, Akbar seemed unconvinced by Birbal's answer. He could not understand how the woman could even touch the ugly child without being even slightly repulsed.

Seeing the Emperor deep in thought, Birbal ordered the palace guard to get the most beautiful child in the world.

The next day the guard got an even uglier child. The poor boy had buck teeth, dark skin and unruly hair that stood like those of a porcupine.

The guard stammered in front of the Emperor, "Your highness, this is the most beautiful child in the world..."

Akbar said, "Really? Who told you so?"

"You see, I went home and posed the question to my wife. She simply pointed to our child and told me to take him to the court."

# Birbal's Flattering Answer

One day, after having an audience with Emperor Akbar, Birbal was going back when a coin fell out of his pocket. He bent down and started searching for it.

Taking this as an opportunity to humiliate the clever man, one of the courtiers said to Akbar, "Look, oh wise Emperor, what a miser Birbal is.

You have given him so much yet he looks around for a single copper coin!"

Birbal smiled and quietly replied, "Sir, it is not the coin that I am worried about, it is the imprint of your face on that coin. I am looking for it so that no one steps on it by mistake!"

Laughing loudly, Akbar said, "You really are quite clever, Birbal!" and gave Birbal his diamond ring.

# The Noble Beggar

Once, Akbar asked Birbal, whether it was possible for someone to be the lowest and the noblest at the same time.

Nodding his head, Birbal said, "Of course your majesty, it is possible."

"Then show it to me," Akbar commanded Birbal.

The next day, Birbal got a beggar to Akbar's court.

"Who is this, Birbal?" Akbar asked.

"Your Majesty, this is the noblest and the lowest person of your kingdom. He is a beggar, therefore your lowest subject, and since he has been given a special audience with the Emperor himself, that makes him the noblest!" said Birbal smiling.

# Fast Horse

One day, as Birbal was sitting outside his house, he saw his dear friend, Hodja, coming on foot towards him. "Hodja!" Birbal called out.

"Oh Birbal, its you!"

"Hodja, you really need a fine horse my friend," Birbal said to him.

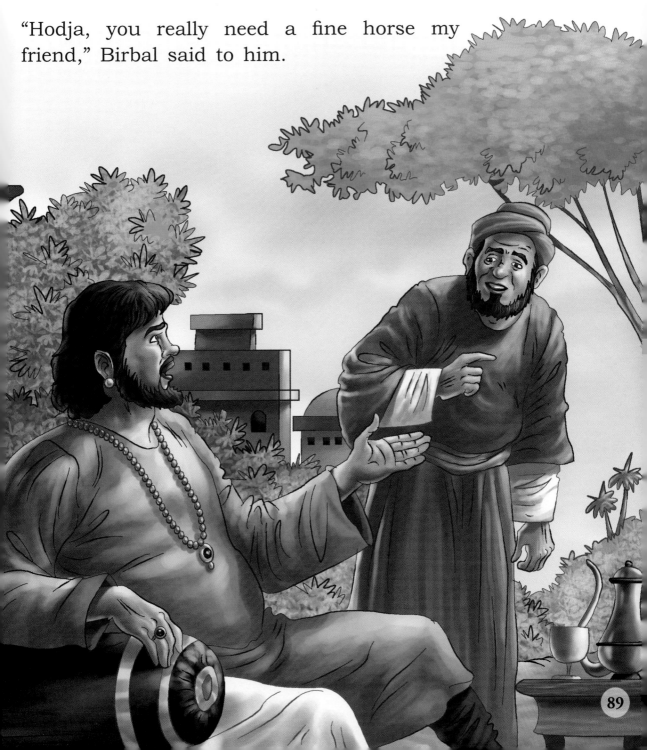

"I know, but what can I do? I do not have enough money to buy a good, sturdy horse…"

"Don't worry, I will get you one," Birbal promised Hodja.

The next day, Birbal instructed his stable man to send a good horse from his stables to Hodja. Now it so happened, that the stable man sent the weakest and the oldest horse to Hodja. It was so weak that the day it reached Hodja, it died the same night.

A week later, Birbal saw Hodja again coming on foot, towards him.

"Why are you on foot, Hodja? What happened to the horse I sent you?"

"Birbal, the horse you sent me was indeed a fast one. It made the journey from Earth to heaven in just a night."

Birbal understood immediately what had happened. He bowed his face in shame and said, "Forgive me, I will immediately get another one sent." And he did.

# The Loyal Gardener

One day, Akbar was strolling in his garden. His mood was already quite bad, when he stumbled and fell on a rock. In sudden anger, he immediately called on his gardener and sentenced him to execution.

And so the poor innocent gardener was sent to jail. As Birbal saw this, he became very sad, but he knew that the Emperor did not mean it.

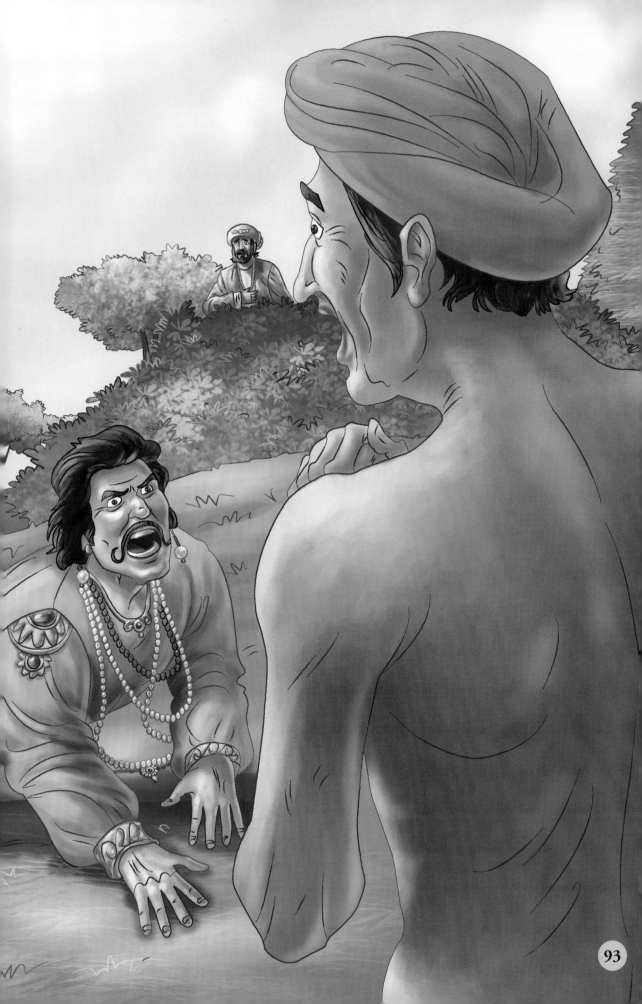

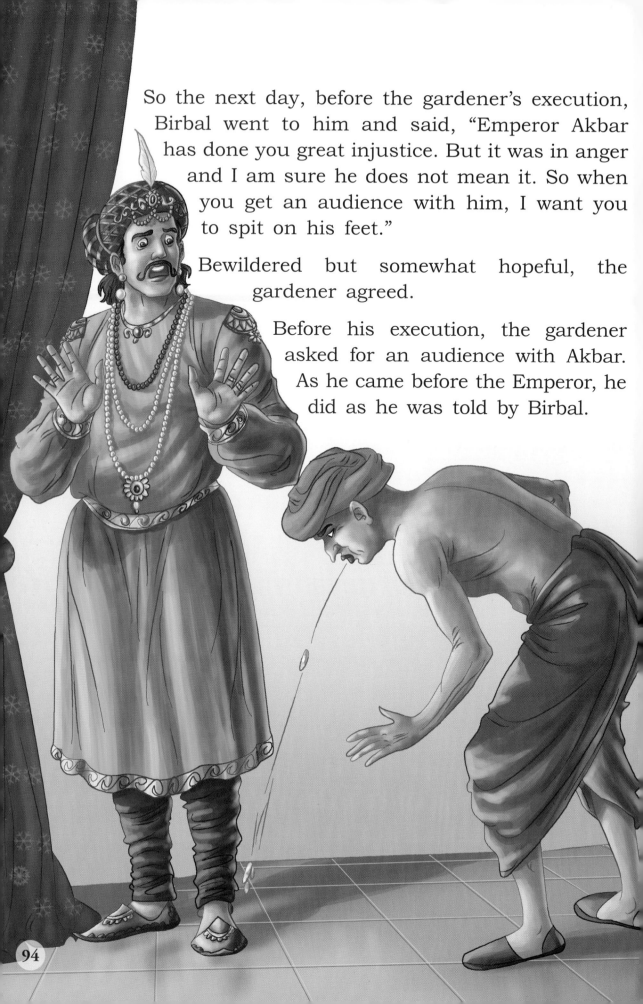

So the next day, before the gardener's execution, Birbal went to him and said, "Emperor Akbar has done you great injustice. But it was in anger and I am sure he does not mean it. So when you get an audience with him, I want you to spit on his feet."

Bewildered but somewhat hopeful, the gardener agreed.

Before his execution, the gardener asked for an audience with Akbar. As he came before the Emperor, he did as he was told by Birbal.

White with rage, Akbar asked the gardener, why he had spit on his feet.

"Your Majesty, Birbal had told me to do so," replied the gardener nervously.

Birbal immediately stepped in and explained himself. "You see, the man who has been sentenced to death is innocent and has been your most faithful servant. He did not want the people to think that you would sentence an innocent man to death in mere rage, so he spat on you. Now you have an actual reason!"

Akbar immediately realised what Birbal meant. He apologised to the gardener and took him back into his service.

# Poet Raidas

In the town of Agra, there lived a rich businessman. But he was also quite a miser. Various people used to flock outside his house everyday, hoping for some kind of generosity, but they always had to return home disappointed. He used to ward them off with false promises and then never live up to his word.

One day, a poet named Raidas arrived at his house and said that he wanted to read out his poems to the rich man. As the rich man was very fond of poetry, he welcomed him with open arms.

Raidas started to recite all his poems, one by one. The rich man was very pleased and especially so when he heard the poem that Raidas had written on him, because he had been compared with 'Kuber', the god of wealth.

In those days it was customary for rich men and kings to show their appreciation through a reward or a gift, as that was the only means of earning that a poor poet possessed. So the rich man promised Raidas some gifts and asked him to come and collect them the next day. Raidas was pleased.

The next morning when he arrived at the house, the rich man pretended not to recognise him. When Raidas reminded him of his promise, he said he did not remember any such thing.

Raidas was extremely upset, but as there was nothing that he could do, he quietly left the house. On his way home, he saw Birbal. So, he stopped him and asked for his help, after narrating the whole incident.

Birbal took him to his own house, in order to come up with a plan. After giving it some thought, he asked Raidas to go to a friend's house and request him to plan a dinner on the coming full-moon night, where the rich man should also be invited. Birbal then asked Raidas to leave the rest to him.

Raidas had one trustworthy friend whose name was Mayadas. So he went up to him and told him the plan. The next day, Mayadas went to the rich man's house and invited him for dinner. The dinner has been planned for the coming

full-moon night. He said that he intended to serve his guests in vessels of gold, which the guests would get to take home after the meal. The rich man was thrilled to hear this and jumped at the invitation.

On the full-moon night, the rich man arrived at Mayadas' house and was surprised to see no other guests there but Raidas. Anyhow, they welcomed him and started a polite conversation. The rich man had come on an empty stomach and so was getting hungrier. Raidas and Mayadas were quite full as they had eaten just before the rich man's arrival.

Finally at midnight, the rich man could bear his hunger no longer and asked Mayadas to serve the food. Mayadas sounded extremely surprised, when he asked him what food was he talking about. The rich man tried to remind him that he had been invited for dinner. At this point Raidas asked him for proof of the invitation. The rich man had no answer.

Then Mayadas told him that he had just invited him to please him and had not really meant it.

At that point Birbal walked into the room and reminded the rich man of the treatment that he had given to Raidas. The rich man realised his mistake and begged for forgiveness.

He said that Raidas was a good poet and had not asked him for any reward. He himself had promised to give him some gifts and then cheated him out of them.

To make up for his mistake, he took off the necklace that he was wearing and gifted it to Raidas. Then they all sat down to eat a happy meal.

# The Three Questions

King Akbar was very fond of Birbal. This made many courtiers very jealous. One day one of the courtiers got an idea. He said that the Emperor praised Birbal unjustly and if Birbal could answer his three questions, he would accept the fact that Birbal was the most intelligent of all courtiers. Akbar agreed.

The three questions were:

1. How many stars are there in the sky?

2. Where is the centre of the Earth?

3. How many men and how many women were there in the world?

Immediately, Akbar asked Birbal these three questions and instructed him that if he could not answer them, he would have to resign from his position in the court.

To answer the first question, Birbal brought a sheep and said, "There are as many stars in the sky as there is hair on this sheep's body. My friend, the courtier, is welcome to count them if he likes."

To answer the second question, Birbal drew a couple of lines on the floor and fixed an iron rod in the middle and said, "This is the centre of the Earth; the courtier may measure it himself if he doubts."

In answer to the third question, Birbal said, "Counting the exact number of men and women in the world would be a problem, as there are some specimens like our courtier friend here, who cannot easily be classified as either. Therefore if all people like him are killed, then and only then can one count the exact number of men and women."

Akbar was very happy with the answers, and the jealous courtier went away without saying a word.

# Fear is the Key

One day King Akbar said to Birbal, "Birbal, my people are very obedient to me. They love me very much."

Birbal smiled and replied, "This is true, but they fear you too, Your Majesty."

Akbar did not agree on this, so it was decided that Birbal's statement should be tested.

Next day, according to Birbal's instructions, the King announced that he would be going for hunting, and people should pour a jug of milk in a tub, kept in the royal courtyard.

A day later, when Akbar returned from hunting, he found that there was no milk in the tub, instead there was only water. He was very disappointed, but could not do anything.

Then Birbal said, "This time you will announce that you will come back and see the tub yourself." The King did as Birbal said. Once again the tub was kept in the royal courtyard.

This time when Akbar returned from hunting, he found the tub overflowing with milk.

Birbal said, "I told you. It is your fear which made people obey you. The first time there was no one to check the tub, so people poured water; but the second time, they knew that you would check yourself, that is why they poured milk."

# Lost Teeth

One night, Emperor Akbar dreamt that he had lost all his teeth, except one. The next morning, he invited all the astrologers of his kingdom to interpret this dream.

After a long discussion, the astrologers declared that all his relatives would die before him. Akbar was very upset by this interpretation and so sent away all the astrologers without any reward.

Later that day, Birbal entered the court. Akbar related his dream and asked him to interpret it.

After thinking for a while, Birbal replied that the Emperor would live a longer and more fulfilled life than any of his relatives.

Akbar was pleased with Birbal's explanation and rewarded him handsomely.

# The Cock's Egg

Since Birbal always outwitted him, Akbar thought of a plan to make Birbal look like a fool. He gave one egg to each of his ministers, before Birbal reached the court, one morning.

When Birbal arrived, the King narrated a dream he had had the previous night, saying that he would be able to judge the sincerity of his ministers, only if they were able to bring back an egg from the royal pond.

Akbar then asked all his courtiers to go to the pond, one at a time and return with an egg. So, one by one, all his ministers went to the pond and returned with the egg which he had previously given to them.

Then it was Birbal's turn. He jumped into the pond and could find no eggs. He realised that the King was trying to play a trick on him. So he entered the court crowing like a cock.

The Emperor asked him to stop making noise and asked him for the egg. Birbal smiled and replied that only hens lay eggs, and as he was a cock, he could not produce an egg.

Everyone laughed loudly and the King realised that Birbal could never easily be fooled.

# The Speed of Sun

As usual, a lot of people were present in Akbar's court, as a famous astrologer had come from a far away country. He was talking about the Solar System and the Earth.

Akbar remarked, "If the Earth is round, and if one travels straight in one direction, he will come back to the same spot from where he has started the journey."

"Theoretically it is correct, but not in real life," said the astrologer.

"Why not in real life?" asked the King.

"One has to cross oceans, mountains and forests to keep the path straight," the astrologer said.

"Sail through the oceans, make tunnels in the mountains and use elephants to cross the forests." Akbar found the solution.

"Still it is impossible," said the astrologer.

"Why?" asked Akbar.

"It may take years to complete the whole journey," said the astrologer.

"How many years?" asked Akbar.

"I don't know. Maybe a hundred years or even more," said the astrologer.

"I will ask my ministers. They have an answer for everything."
Akbar looked at the ministers to get the answer.

"Impossible to calculate."

"Around 25 years."

"Fifty years or less."

"80 days."

"Why Birbal, you haven't uttered a word!" The King showed
his surprise at Birbal's silence.

"I was just calculating the time required to go around the Earth," explained Birbal.

"And did you get the answer?" asked the King.

"Sure," said Birbal, "it will take just one day."

"Just one day! Birbal, it is impossible! It takes more than one day to cross our own country," said Akbar.

"It is possible. Provided you travel at the speed of the Sun!" said Birbal with a smile.

# Pandit Sevaram

One day, a Brahmin by the name of Sevaram, asked Birbal for help. He said that his forefathers were great Sanskrit scholars and that people used to respectfully refer to them as Panditji.

He said that he had no money nor need for wealth; he was content living a simple life. But he had just one wish. He wished that people would refer to him as Panditji too. He wanted Birbal to help him achieve this.

Birbal said that the task was fairly simple. If the Brahmin followed his advice word for word, this task could be achieved. Birbal advised the Brahmin to shout at anyone who would call him Panditji from then on.

Now the children who lived on the same street as the Brahmin did not like him, since he scolded them often. They were just waiting for an opportunity to get back at him. Birbal told the children that the Brahmin would get really irritated if they would start calling him Panditji. The children loved this piece of information and started calling the Brahmin "Panditji."

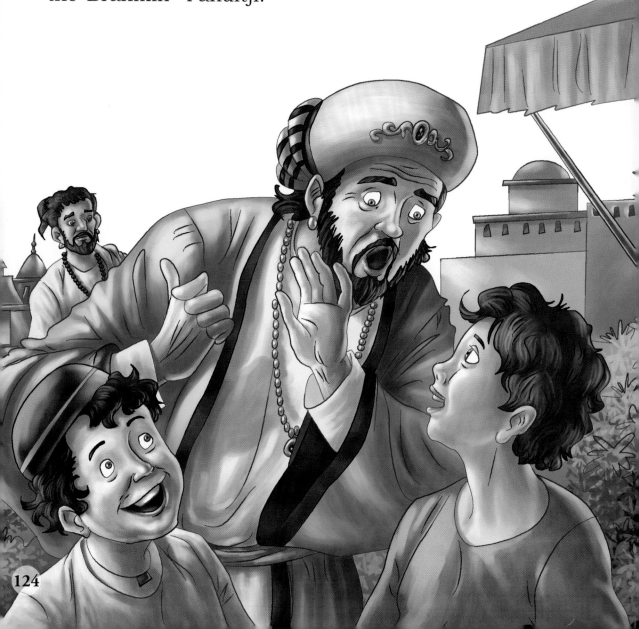

And the Brahmin, as advised by Birbal, started shouting at them. The children spread the word to all the other children in the neighbourhood that Sevaram hated being called Panditji, so the entire neighbourhood started calling him Panditji.

After a while, Sevaram got tired of scolding them but everyone had become used to calling him Panditji.

Birbal's plan worked, and the name stuck.

# A Little Less and a Little More

Once, Birbal brought his five year old daughter to the royal court with him. When Akbar saw her, he wanted to see if she had her father's wit. So he asked her a question.

"Little girl, do you know Persian?" Akbar asked her.

"A little less and a little more sir," Birbal's daughter answered.

Birbal smiling at his daughter, explained, "What she means by this is that she knows lesser Persian than the ones who speak Persian, and more than those who do not speak the language."

Akbar was quite pleased by Birbal's daughter's answer. He said to Birbal, "I see that she has indeed got your wit Birbal. She would grow up to be a clever woman!"